95 QUESTIONS A SINGLE MOM MUST ASK HERSELF BEFORE GOING BACK TO DATING AGAIN

EVERYTHING SHE MUST ASK HERSELF TO AVOID DATING THE WRONG PERSON AND LOSING EVERYTHING YOU'VE WORKED FOR

DISCLAIMER

This book is designed to provide information only. This information is provided and sold with the knowledge that the publisher and author do not offer any legal or other professional advice. In the case of a need for any such expertise, consult with the appropriate professional.

This book does not contain all the information available on the subject. This book has not been created to be specific to any individual's or organization's situation or needs. Every effort has been made to make this book as accurate as possible. However, there may be typographical and or content errors. Therefore, this book should serve only as a general guide, not as the ultimate source of subject information.

This book contains information that might be dated and is intended only to educate and entertain. The author and publisher shall have no liability or responsibility to any person or entity regarding any loss or damage incurred or alleged to have incurred, directly or indirectly, by the information contained in this book.

Table of Contents

Introduction

Welcome to "Back to the Dating World: 95 Questions a Single Mom Must Ask Herself," – a comprehensive guide designed to support single moms embarking on the exhilarating and sometimes challenging journey of dating once again.

As you hold this book in your hands, you're about to embark on a transformative exploration of self-discovery, empowerment, and personal growth.

Dating as a single mom can be both exciting and daunting. It's a chance to rediscover yourself, embrace new connections, and potentially find a loving partner who complements your life and supports your family.

However, the path forward can also be filled with uncertainties and questions that arise when blending the worlds of parenting and romance.

In this book, we present you with a curated collection of 95 thought-provoking questions specifically crafted for single moms like you. These questions are designed to delve deep into your desires, values, and aspirations, allowing you to gain clarity, set boundaries, and make informed decisions as you navigate the dating landscape.

Whether you are considering a serious commitment or simply seeking companionship, this book will guide you on the path to fulfilling relationships while prioritizing the well-being of both you and your children.

Each question acts as a compass, gently nudging you toward self-reflection and empowering you to make choices that align with your authentic self. From introspective inquiries about emotional readiness and deal-breakers to practical considerations about blending families and balancing responsibilities, these prompts cover a wide range of topics, addressing the complexities and nuances unique to single motherhood.

Take your time with these questions. Dive into them with honesty, vulnerability, and an open heart. The answers you uncover will illuminate your desires, clarify your expectations, and empower you to navigate the dating world with confidence and self-assurance.

Remember, this journey is about rediscovering your own worth, building a strong foundation for yourself and your children, and attracting the love and support you deserve.

So, take a deep breath, open your heart, and let the exploration begin. The possibilities that await you are boundless, and these 95 questions will be your trusted companions, guiding you toward a future filled with love, joy, and personal growth.

So, get ready to dive in, answer the questions that resonate with you, and embark on an empowering journey of self-discovery.

The world of dating is yours to explore, and you are ready to embrace it fully.

The FAQ You Need To Understand What "DASM" Is Really About

1. Is it possible to find love as a single mom?

Absolutely! Being a single mom doesn't mean you can't find love. Many single moms have successful and fulfilling relationships. It may require patience, open communication, and finding a partner who understands and supports your unique situation.

2. How do I balance dating with my responsibilities as a single mom?

Balancing dating with parenting responsibilities can be a challenge. It's important to prioritize self-care and ensure that your children's needs are met.

Establish clear boundaries, communicate openly with your partner about your schedule, and seek support from friends and family when needed.

3. When is the right time to introduce my children to a new partner?

There's no one-size-fits-all answer. The timing will depend on various factors, including the stability of the relationship and the readiness of both you and your children.

It's generally recommended to wait until the relationship is serious and you believe your partner will be a long-term presence in your children's lives.

4. How do I handle potential conflicts between my children and my new partner?

Open communication is key. Encourage your children to express their feelings and concerns, and listen to their perspectives. Foster positive interactions and give everyone time to adjust. Patience, understanding, and setting clear boundaries can help navigate conflicts and create a harmonious family dynamic.

5. What if my potential partner doesn't want to be involved with my children?

It's essential to be upfront about your status as a single mom from the beginning. If a potential partner is not interested in being involved with your children, it's important to respect their decision and consider whether that aligns with your long-term goals and values.

It's crucial to find a partner who supports and embraces your role as a parent.

6. How can I deal with judgment or negative reactions from others about my single mom status?

Unfortunately, judgment from others may occur, but remember that your happiness and well-being matter most. Surround yourself with supportive friends and family who uplift you. Focus on your own journey, ignore negativity, and prioritize the opinions of those who truly understand and respect your choices.

7. Should I disclose my single mom status on dating profiles?

It's a personal decision. Some single moms prefer to mention their children on their dating profiles to be transparent from the start.

Others choose to disclose this information later when a connection is established. Do what feels right for you and aligns with your comfort level.

8. How can I find time for dating as a busy single mom?

Time management and prioritization are crucial. Consider outsourcing or delegating certain tasks to create free time for dating. Utilize childcare resources, establish a support system, and communicate your needs with your partner. Efficient scheduling and self-care can help you make time for your dating life.

9. How do I handle potential insecurities or fears related to dating as a single mom?

Insecurities and fears are common, but it's essential to remember your worth. Embrace self-love and work on building your confidence. Surround yourself with supportive people who uplift you.

Be patient and give yourself time to heal from any past experiences. Therapy or counseling can also be beneficial in addressing these concerns.

10. How do I know if a potential partner is right for me and my children?

Trust your instincts and pay attention to how a potential partner interacts with you and your children. Look for someone who shows understanding, respect, and genuine interest in your family. Open and honest communication about expectations, values, and parenting styles is vital in determining compatibility.

11. How do I handle potential conflicts between my ex-partner and my new partner?

Clear and respectful communication is key. Set boundaries with both your ex-partner and new partner, and encourage open dialogue. Keep the focus on the well-being of your children and strive for a harmonious coexistence.

12. What if I feel guilty about dating and taking time for myself?

It's common to experience feelings of guilt when prioritizing your own happiness. Remember that taking care of yourself is essential for your well-being and sets a positive example for your children. Embrace self-care without guilt, knowing that it benefits both you and your family.

13. How can I navigate dating with limited financial resources?

Dating doesn't have to be expensive. Look for low-cost or free activities, such as picnics in the park, hiking, or exploring local attractions. Openly communicate your financial situation with your partner, and focus on building a connection based on shared values and experiences rather than material possessions.

14. How do I handle potential differences in parenting styles with a new partner?

Open communication is crucial. Discuss your parenting styles, values, and expectations early on in the relationship. Find common ground and seek compromise when necessary. Respect each other's perspectives and work together to create a cohesive and supportive parenting approach.

15. Should I introduce my children to every person I date?

It's generally advisable to introduce your children to someone new only when you feel the relationship has long-term potential. Introducing them too soon can create confusion and instability.

Prioritize their emotional well-being and ensure that your relationship is stable and committed before involving them.

16. How can I manage the emotional impact of dating and potential rejections?

Rejections can be tough, but remember that it's not a reflection of your worth. Practice self-compassion and maintain a positive mindset. Surround yourself with supportive friends and family who uplift you. Focus on personal growth, and trust that the right person will come into your life at the right time.

17. How do I establish boundaries regarding my dating life and my children?

Boundaries are crucial to ensure your and your children's well-being. Communicate openly with your partner about your expectations and concerns. Set aside dedicated time for dating and separate it from your parenting responsibilities.

Prioritize quality time with your children and establish rules around introducing partners to maintain stability.

18. What if I feel hesitant about blending families or introducing a new partner to my children?

It's natural to have concerns and reservations. Take the time to establish a strong foundation in your relationship before introducing your children. Trust your instincts and only take this step when you're confident in the commitment and potential long-term compatibility.

19. How do I handle potential judgment from potential partners who may not be open to dating a single mom?

Remember that not everyone will be compatible with your situation, and that's okay. Focus on finding someone who appreciates and embraces your role as a single mom. Be confident in who you are and the value you bring to a relationship.

20. Should I involve my children in the decision-making process regarding my dating life?

Depending on their age and maturity level, it can be helpful to include your children in discussions about dating. Consider their thoughts and feelings, but ultimately, as the parent, you have the final say in determining the course of your dating life.

21. How can I prioritize self-care while balancing dating and parenting responsibilities?

Self-care is essential to maintain your well-being. Set aside dedicated time for yourself, engage in activities that bring you joy, and seek support from friends or family when needed. Remember that taking care of yourself allows you to be the best version of yourself for your children and potential partners.

22. How do I address concerns about my children getting attached to a new partner who may not become a long-term presence in their lives?

Be honest and transparent with your children about the nature of your relationship and potential changes. Encourage open communication and reassure them that their feelings are valid. Take it slow and prioritize their emotional well-being throughout the process.

23. What if I'm hesitant about trusting someone new after a past relationship or marriage?

It's natural to have trust concerns after a difficult experience. Take your time to build trust with a new partner. Communicate your fears and concerns, and give yourself permission to heal. Engage in self-reflection and seek support from a therapist or counselor if needed.

24. How can I navigate potential cultural or religious differences with a new partner?

Open and respectful communication is crucial. Discuss your beliefs, values, and traditions early on in the relationship. Seek to understand and appreciate each other's perspectives. Find common ground and be willing to compromise when necessary.

25. What if I feel overwhelmed by the dating process and balancing multiple responsibilities?

It's important to recognize and address feelings of overwhelm. Prioritize self-care, establish clear boundaries, and ask for help when needed. Consider seeking support from support groups, therapists, or online communities specifically for single moms.

Remember, the dating journey as a single mom is unique to each individual. Trust your instincts, prioritize your well-being and that of your children, and be patient with yourself.

With self-reflection, open communication, and self-care, you can navigate the dating world and find a fulfilling and loving relationship.

How To Get The Most Out Of These Questions?

Here are some suggestions to get the most out of these questions:

1. Set aside dedicated time:

Create a quiet and comfortable space to focus on self-reflection without distractions. Set aside dedicated time to work through the questions at your own pace.

2. Approach with an open mind:

Be open to exploring different aspects of yourself and your desires. Allow yourself to think deeply and honestly, even if some questions may initially feel challenging or uncomfortable.

3. Journal your responses:

Consider journaling your answers to each question. Writing down your thoughts allows for greater clarity and provides a record of your journey. It also enables you to reflect on your progress over time.

4. Take breaks when needed:

It's important to recognize that self-reflection can sometimes be emotionally intense. If you feel overwhelmed or need a break, allow yourself time to process your thoughts and emotions before continuing.

5. Embrace vulnerability:

Honesty and vulnerability are key to gaining the most value from the questions. Challenge yourself to dig deep and explore your true thoughts and feelings. This is an opportunity for personal growth and self-discovery.

6. Reflect on your answers:

After answering each question, take a moment to reflect on your responses. Consider how they align with your values, goals, and the life you envision for yourself and your children. Use this reflection to guide your decisions and actions moving forward.

7. Seek support if needed:

If certain questions trigger strong emotions or bring up unresolved issues, consider seeking support from a therapist, counselor, or trusted friend. They can provide guidance and help you navigate any challenges that arise.

8. Create an action plan:

As you progress through the questions, identify patterns, themes, and areas where you'd like to make changes or set boundaries. Then, develop an action plan to implement the insights you gain into your dating journey and overall well-being.

9. Celebrate your progress:

Acknowledge and celebrate your growth along the way. Recognize that every step you take, and every question you answer, brings you closer to a more fulfilling and authentic life.

Remember, this book is a tool to support your self-discovery and empower you in your dating journey as a single mom.

The questions are meant to be thought-provoking and assist you in making informed decisions that align with your values, desires, and the well-being of your family.

So enjoy the process, embrace the journey, and trust in your own wisdom as you navigate the exciting world of dating once again.

95 Questions A Single Mom Must Ask Herself Before Going Back To Dating Again

Entering the dating world as a single mom can bring up a lot of questions and considerations.

Here are 95 questions that a single mom might find helpful to ask herself as she navigates this new chapter in her life.

1. Am I emotionally ready to start dating again?

2. What are my priorities in a potential partner?

3. Am I looking for a long-term relationship or something more casual?

4. How will dating affect my children?

5. What boundaries do I need to set when it comes to introducing my children to someone new?

6. What qualities and values are important to me in a partner?

7. Am I open to dating someone who doesn't have children?

8. How will I balance my time between dating and parenting?

9. What are my deal-breakers when it comes to dating?

10. How will I handle potential rejection or disappointment?

11. Am I financially stable enough to pursue a relationship?

12. Do I have a strong support system in place to help me with parenting and dating?

13. How will I navigate conversations about my past relationship or marriage?

14. Am I ready to trust someone new after my previous relationship?

15. What are my expectations when it comes to communication and availability from a partner?

16. How will I handle potential conflicts or disagreements with a new partner?

17. Am I comfortable discussing my children with a potential partner?

18. How will I prioritize self-care while dating as a single mom?

19. What are my long-term goals when it comes to dating and relationships?

20. Am I open to dating someone with different religious or cultural beliefs?

21. How will I handle any negative reactions or judgments from others about my single mom status?

22. What are my boundaries when it comes to physical intimacy in a new relationship?

23. Am I ready to let someone new into my children's lives?

24. What lessons have I learned from my previous relationship or marriage?

25. How will I handle potential conflicts between my children and a new partner?

26. Am I prepared for the potential challenges of blending families?

27. What type of support am I seeking from a partner?

28. How will I balance my personal needs with the needs of my children in a new relationship?

29. Am I open to dating someone who lives in a different location?

30. How will I handle potential jealousy or insecurity in a new relationship?

31. What are my expectations around parenting roles and responsibilities in a new relationship?

32. Am I willing to compromise in a relationship and make adjustments for my partner and children?

33. How will I handle potential differences in parenting styles with a new partner?

34. What are my plans for future family dynamics if the relationship becomes serious?

35. Am I open to the possibility of having more children with a new partner?

36. How will I handle potential changes in my lifestyle and routines with a new partner?

37. What are my expectations around financial contributions and responsibilities in a new relationship?

38. Am I ready to share my personal space and belongings with a new partner?

39. How will I handle potential conflicts between my ex-partner and a new partner?

40. What are my expectations around the involvement of my ex-partner in my dating life?

41. Am I willing to consider a long-distance relationship?

42. How will I handle potential differences in values or beliefs with a new partner?

43. What role will my children play in the decision-making process regarding a new relationship?

44. Am I comfortable with the idea of dating someone who has children from a previous relationship?

45. How will I handle potential changes in my career or work-life balance with a new partner?

46. What are my boundaries when it comes to social media and online presence in a new relationship?

47. Am I open to dating someone who has been divorced or has had previous relationships?

48. How will I handle potential changes in my social circle or friendships with a new partner?

49. What are my expectations around shared activities and hobbies in a new relationship?

50. Am I ready to let go of any lingering resentments or emotional baggage from my past relationship?

51. How will I handle potential changes in my living arrangements with a new partner?

52. What role will my children play in determining the pace of the relationship?

53. Am I willing to seek professional help or counseling if needed during the dating process?

54. How will I handle potential changes in my parenting style or decisions with a new partner?

55. What are my expectations around privacy and personal space in a new relationship?

56. Am I open to dating someone with a significant age difference?

57. How will I handle potential changes in my personal goals or aspirations with a new partner?

58. What are my boundaries when it comes to involvement with my ex-partner's family?

59. Am I comfortable with the idea of my children forming attachments to a new partner?

60. How will I handle potential changes in my travel plans or lifestyle with a new partner?

61. What are my expectations around emotional support and communication in a new relationship?

62. Am I open to dating someone who has different political views?

63. How will I handle potential changes in my children's routines or schedules with a new partner?

64. What role will my children play in the decision-making process regarding marriage or commitment?

65. Am I ready to fully embrace the dating experience and all that it entails?

66. How will I handle potential changes in my holiday traditions or celebrations with a new partner?

67. What are my expectations around trust and loyalty in a new relationship?

68. Am I willing to make adjustments to my lifestyle or living situation for a new partner?

69. How will I handle potential differences in communication styles with a new partner?

70. What are my boundaries when it comes to discussing my ex-partner with a new partner?

71. Am I open to dating someone who has different parenting styles or approaches?

72. How will I handle potential changes in my financial situation or responsibilities with a new partner?

73. What role will my children play in the decision-making process regarding moving in together?

74. Am I comfortable with the idea of dating someone with a different cultural background?

75. How will I handle potential differences in social activities or preferences with a new partner?

76. What are my expectations around personal growth and self-improvement in a new relationship?

77. Am I open to dating someone with a different education or career background?

78. How will I handle potential changes in my healthcare or insurance arrangements with a new partner?

79. What role will my children play in the decision-making process regarding marriage or commitment?

80. Am I willing to make adjustments to my lifestyle or living situation for a new partner?

81. How will I handle potential differences in communication styles with a new partner?

82. Am I open to dating someone who has different parenting styles or approaches?

83. What role will my children play in the decision-making process regarding moving in together?

84. Am I comfortable with the idea of dating someone with a different cultural background?

85. How will I handle potential differences in social activities or preferences with a new partner?

86. What are my expectations around personal growth and self-improvement in a new relationship?

87. Am I open to dating someone with a different education or career background?

88. How will I handle potential changes in my healthcare or insurance arrangements with a new partner?

89. What role will my children play in the decision-making process regarding marriage or commitment?

90. Am I willing to make adjustments to my lifestyle or living situation for a new partner?

91. How will I handle potential differences in communication styles with a new partner?

92. Am I open to dating someone who has different parenting styles or approaches?

93. What role will my children play in the decision-making process regarding moving in together?

94. Am I comfortable with the idea of dating someone with a different cultural background?

95. What are my expectations around personal growth and self-improvement in a new relationship?

Conclusion

As you reach the end of "Back to the Dating World: 95 Questions a Single Mom Must Ask Herself," I want to extend my heartfelt gratitude to you for embarking on this journey of self-discovery and personal growth.

Your commitment to exploring these questions and seeking clarity in your life is truly commendable.

I sincerely hope that this book has provided you with valuable insights, empowered you to make informed decisions, and ignited a renewed sense of confidence within you.

By delving deep into your desires, values, and aspirations, you have taken significant steps towards creating a life that aligns with your authentic self and nurtures the well-being of both you and your children.

Your presence as a reader and your engagement with these questions are incredibly valuable. I encourage you to take a moment to leave a review on Amazon, sharing your thoughts and experiences with other potential readers.

Your review has the power to inspire and guide others who may be seeking the same clarity and empowerment you have found through this book.

By leaving a review, you not only support me as an author but also extend a helping hand to fellow single moms who may be yearning for guidance and understanding.

In addition, your words can resonate with those who need to hear this important message and encourage them to embark on their own journey of self-reflection.

Your honest review on Amazon serves as a beacon of light, illuminating the path for others who are searching for clarity in their own lives. It can make a significant difference in helping them discover their desires, set boundaries, and make informed decisions that shape their dating experiences and overall well-being.

Once again, thank you for choosing "Back to the Dating World: 95 Questions a Single Mom Must Ask Herself" and for investing your time and energy into your personal growth. Your commitment to self-discovery is an inspiration, and I am truly grateful to have been a part of your journey.

May your path be filled with love, joy, and the fulfillment of your deepest desires. Remember, you deserve a meaningful and fulfilling life, both as a single mom and as an individual.

So embrace the lessons you've learned, cherish the insights you've gained, and continue to embrace the dating world with confidence, knowing that you are equipped with the tools to create the life you truly deserve.

With the deepest gratitude,

Yakalou

Books By YAKALOU MEDIA

- Questions to Gain Clarity About Your Life
- Questions to Gain Clarity About Your Purpose
- Questions to Gain Clarity About Your Career
- Questions to Ask Yourself to Get Clarity About Your Passions
- Questions to Have Clarity About Your Personal Finance
- Questions to Clarity About Your Relationships with Your Parents
- Questions You Must Ask Yourself When Dating in Your 30s
- 70+ Ways to Ask a Guy or Girl to Be Friends with Benefits (FWB)
- 30 Reasons Why Happily Married Men Cheat
- Questions to Gain Clarity About your Spiritual Beliefs
- Questions to Gain Clarity About Choosing Your Life Partner.
- 100 Questions I Should Ask Myself Before Coming Out
- Questions to Ask Yourself to Get Clarity About Your Mental Health
- Questions To Ask Yourself To Have Clarity About Your Decision-making Process
- Questions To Ask Yourself To Have Clarity About Your Work-life Balance

- 100 Essential Questions to Ask Yourself When Dating in Your Late 20s
- Back to the Dating World: 100 Questions a Single Mom Must Ask Herself
- Questions to Ask Yourself About Sex Addiction When Approaching Your 30s
- 100 Questions to Ask Yourself About Compulsive lying addiction

—Please leave a review!

As always, we value your feedback and would love to read your review of this book!